NIGERIA

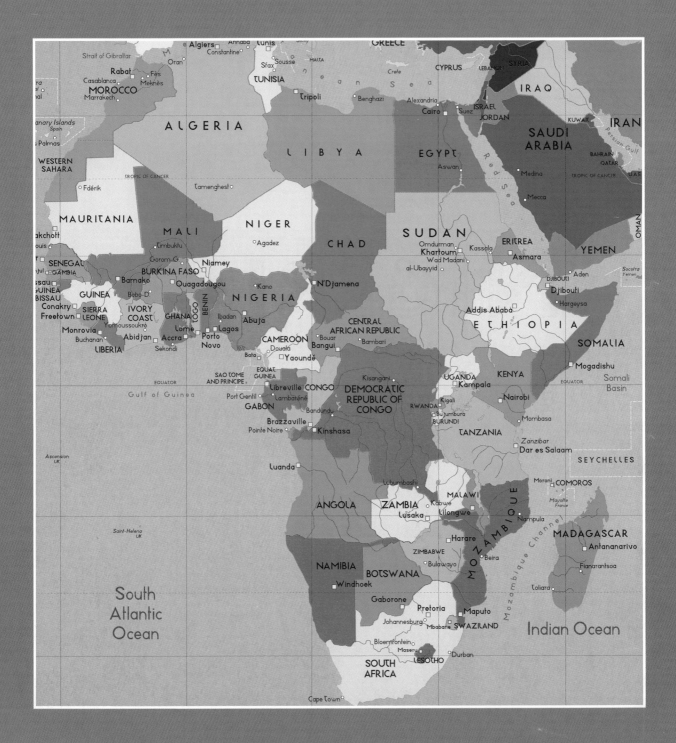

NIGERIA

Ida Walker

Mason Crest Publishers
Philadelphia

Produced by OTTN Publishing, Stockton, N.J.

Mason Crest Publishers
370 Reed Road
Broomall, PA 19008
www.masoncrest.com

3 5 7 9 8 6 4 2

Library of Congress Cataloging-in-Publication Data

Walker, Ida
  Nigeria / Ida Walker.
      p. cm. — (Africa)
  Includes bibliographical references and index.
  ISBN 1-59084-811-X
  1. Nigeria—Juvenile literature. I. Title. II. Series.

DT515.22.W35 2004
966.9—dc22

                                                          2004007100

Table of Contents

Africa: Continent in the Balance
Robert I. Rotberg

Africa is the cradle of humankind, but for millennia it was off the familiar, beaten path of global commerce and discovery. Its many peoples therefore developed largely apart from the diffusion of modern knowledge and the spread of technological innovation until the 17th through 19th centuries. With the coming to Africa of the book, the wheel, the hoe, and the modern rifle and cannon, foreigners also brought the vastly destructive transatlantic slave trade, oppression, discrimination, and onerous colonial rule. Emerging from that crucible of European rule, Africans created nationalistic movements and then claimed their numerous national independences in the 1960s. The result is the world's largest continental assembly of new countries.

There are 53 members of the African Union, a regional political grouping, and 48 of those nations lie south of the Sahara. Fifteen of them, including mighty Ethiopia, are landlocked, making international trade and economic growth that much more arduous and expensive. Access to navigable rivers is limited, natural harbors are few, soils are poor and thin, several countries largely consist of miles and miles of sand, and tropical diseases have sapped the strength and productivity of innumerable millions. Being landlocked, having few resources (although countries along Africa's west coast have tapped into deep offshore petroleum and gas reservoirs), and being beset by malaria, tuberculosis, schistosomiasis, AIDS, and many other maladies has kept much of Africa poor for centuries.

Thirty-two of the world's poorest 44 countries are African. Hunger is common. So is rapid deforestation and desertification. Unemployment rates are often over 50 percent, for jobs are few—even in agriculture. Where Africa once

Africa's most populous country, Nigeria has been a trading center in West Africa for centuries.

was a land of small villages and a few large cities, with almost everyone engaged in growing grain or root crops or grazing cattle, camels, sheep, and goats, today more than half of all the more than 750 million Africans, especially those who live south of the Sahara, reside in towns and cities. Traditional agriculture hardly pays, and a number of countries in Africa—particularly the smaller and more fragile ones—can no longer feed themselves.

There is not one Africa, for the continent is full of contradictions and variety. Of the 675 million people living south of the Sahara, at least 130 million live in Nigeria, 67 million in Ethiopia, 55 million in the Democratic Republic of the

A Yoruba family stands in front of their traditional home. The Yoruba are one of Nigeria's largest ethnic groups and are native to the country's southern region.

Congo, and 45 million in South Africa. By contrast, tiny Djibouti and Equatorial Guinea have fewer than 1 million people each, and prosperous Botswana and Namibia each are under 2 million in population. Within some countries, even medium-sized ones like Zambia (11 million), there are a plethora of distinct ethnic groups speaking separate languages. Zambia, typical with its multitude of competing entities, has 70 such peoples, roughly broken down into four language and cultural zones. Three of those languages jostle with English for primacy.

Given the kaleidoscopic quality of African culture and deep-grained poverty, it is no wonder that Africa has developed economically and politically less rapidly than other regions. Since independence from colonial rule, weak governance has also plagued Africa and contributed significantly to the widespread poverty of its peoples. Only Botswana and offshore Mauritius have been governed democratically without interruption since independence. Both are among Africa's wealthiest countries, too, thanks to the steady application of good governance.

Aside from those two nations, and South Africa, Africa has been a continent of coups since 1960, with massive and oil-rich Nigeria suffering incessant periods of harsh, corrupt, autocratic military rule. Nearly every other country on or around the continent, small and large, has been plagued by similar bouts of instability and dictatorial rule. In the 1970s and 1980s Idi Amin ruled Uganda capriciously and Jean-Bedel Bokassa proclaimed himself emperor of the Central African Republic. Macias Nguema of Equatorial Guinea was another in that same mold. More recently Daniel arap Moi held Kenya in thrall and Robert Mugabe has imposed himself on once-prosperous Zimbabwe. In both of those cases, as in the case of Gnassingbe Eyadema in Togo and the late Mobutu Sese Seko in Congo, these presidents stole wildly and drove entire peoples and their nations into penury. Corruption is common in Africa, and so are a weak rule-of-law framework, misplaced development, high expenditures on soldiers and low expenditures on health and education, and a widespread (but not universal) refusal on the part of leaders to work well for their followers and citizens.

Conflict between groups within countries has also been common in Africa. More than 12 million Africans have been killed in the civil wars of Africa since 1990, with more than 3 million losing their lives in Congo and more than 2 million in the Sudan. War between north and south has been constant in the Sudan since 1981. In 2003 there were serious ongoing hostilities in northeastern Congo, Burundi, Angola, Liberia, Guinea, Ivory Coast, the Central African Republic, and Guinea-Bissau, and a coup (later reversed) in São Tomé and Príncipe.

Despite such dangers, despotism, and decay, Africa is improving. Botswana and Mauritius, now joined by South Africa, Senegal, Kenya, and Ghana, are beacons of democratic growth and enlightened rule. Uganda and Senegal are taking the lead in combating and reducing the spread of AIDS, and others are following. There are serious signs of the kinds of progressive economic policy changes that might lead to prosperity for more of Africa's peoples. The trajectory in Africa is positive.

The Niger River, which flows into the Gulf of Guinea, is one of Nigeria's most valuable natural resources. (Opposite) Here fishermen search for their catch on the river. (Right) Women walk with containers filled from a stream in the Niger Delta.

1 From Desert to Rain Forest

NIGERIA IS AFRICA'S most populous country and one of its most diverse. Over 130 million Nigerians speak 505 languages and practice Christianity, Islam, and indigenous religions. Tribal villages preserve native traditions, while modern cities bolster a national economy that benefits from a plentiful oil supply. This diversity extends to the country's geography, which includes rivers, waterfalls, savannas, rain forests, deserts, beaches, and mountain vistas.

Located in West Africa, Nigeria is a little more than twice the size of California, with a total area of 356,805 square miles (923,768 square kilometers). The country's coastline extends 530 miles (853 km) and runs along the Gulf of Guinea, an inlet of the Atlantic Ocean. The Niger River, which inspired the country's name, flows through the central section of Nigeria and empties into the Gulf of Guinea. Nigeria's neighbors are Niger to the north, Cameroon to the south and east, and Benin to the west.

The Landscape

Most of Nigeria is relatively flat. The higher altitudes—those above 3,940 feet (1,200 meters)—are only found in the Jos Plateau and in mountains running up the eastern border with Cameroon. These mountains contain the country's highest point, Chappal Waddi, which stands at 7,936 feet (2,419 meters).

The coastal plain ranges from 10 to 60 miles (16 to 97 km) wide. Dividing the plain is the Niger Delta, which is mostly covered with mangrove swamps. *Tropical* rain forests cover a large segment of central Nigeria, and are the source of the two of the country's main exports, cocoa and oil palm. North of the rain forests are the *savannas.* The grasslands found in this area are excellent for grazing, and most of the country's meat comes from here. Plateaus and granite mountains are common in the region north of the Niger and Benue river basins, and they also appear in the southwestern part of the country.

Although much of Nigeria is flat, there are a few areas boasting impressive features that draw tourists and adventurers. Caves, rocky hills, and scenic waterfalls are all found along the Ogun River in southwest Nigeria. The Ogbunike caves and Agulu Lake are located in the southeast. More waterfalls are found in central Nigeria, as are the Chukuku Hills, the Agwai Hills, and the Zuma rocks. Perhaps this region's most fantastic feature is Jos Plateau, popular for the view it provides of the surrounding land. Assop Falls and Riyom Rock, located outside the city of Jos, are other landmarks popular with tourists and residents alike.

Standing in contrast to the landscape of the southern and central regions are the northwest's sand dunes and oases, which are especially prominent during the dry season. Lush growth appears here during the region's long rainy season.

Climate

Nigeria's climate varies by region. It is *equatorial* in the south, tropical in the central region, and arid in the north. There are basically two seasons—dry and rainy. In the north, the rainy season lasts from April until September;

Quick Facts: The Geography of Nigeria

Location: Western Africa, bordering the Gulf of Guinea, between Benin and Cameroon

Area: (slightly more than twice the size of California)
total: 356,874 square miles (923,768 sq km)
land: 351,556 square miles (910,768 sq km)
water: 5,018 square miles (13,000 sq km)

Borders: Benin, 480 miles (773 km); Cameroon, 1,050 miles (1,690 km); Chad, 54 miles (87 km); Niger, 930 miles (1,497 km); coastline, 530 miles (853 km)

Climate: varies; equatorial in south, tropical in center, arid in north

Terrain: southern lowlands merge into central hills and plateaus; mountains in southeast, plains in north

Elevation extremes:
lowest point: Atlantic Ocean, 0 feet
highest point: Chappal Waddi, 7,936 feet (2,419 meters)

Natural hazards: periodical droughts; flooding

Source: Adapted from CIA World Factbook, 2003.

in the south, it begins earlier, in March, and ends as late as November. The average rainfall along the Gulf of Guinea is considerably higher than in other areas. The coastal city of Lagos, for example, receives an average of 75 inches (190 cm) of rain per year, while just 100 miles (160 km) to the north, average rainfall levels only total about 49 inches (125 cm), and in the northern region, they fall between 20 and 30 inches (50 and 75 cm).

Temperatures above 90°F (32°C) are common in the northern region. The central region of the country has a climate that allows for year-round plant growth as long as the water supply is adequate. Toward the south, where it is typically hot and humid, temperatures range from 73°F to 88°F (23°C to 31°C). The cooler December and January winds that come from the desert offer a break from the humidity.

Animals

Nigeria is home to many animals that are also common to other parts of Africa, including antelope, jackals, hyenas, hippopotamus, and elephants. Animals native to Nigeria include the Hercules Baboon tarantula and two types of monkeys: the red-capped mangabey and the mona guenon.

Nigeria's tropical rain forest is home to the red-capped mangabey, also called the cherry-crowned, or white-collared, mangabey. This monkey has a dark face and white eyelids and weighs between 15 and 20 pounds (6.8 and 11.3 kilograms). It uses its eyelids as a signaling tool to socialize with other mangabeys, and has large cheek pouches to store food. The mona guenon, a monkey with a tail twice the length of its body, lives in Nigeria's mangrove forests.

Environmental Issues

Nigeria's environment suffers from many of the same problems affecting other African countries on or near the equator. Both flooding and droughts have always been serious threats, and experts report that the 20th century was one of the driest centuries for Nigeria on record.

Perhaps what are more problematic than the naturally occurring hazards are those that humans have caused. Nigeria's most serious environmental problems are greatly attributed to the oil industry, upon which Nigeria is economically dependent. Oil spills have caused serious, long-lasting damage to the water and the soil.

A boy stands beside a sign indicating that the water is polluted with oil. Nigeria's oil industry contributes greatly to the national economy, but is also responsible for contaminating much of the soil and the water.

Other environmental issues that Nigeria is presently dealing with are deforestation, urban air and water pollution, *desertification*, and the loss of usable land for crops. Although some of these problems can be traced directly to the oil industry, others are partly due to the rapid growth of the country's population. In short, there are too many people trying to fit in an area that is too small for them all. As a result, forests and agricultural land are being stripped to make room for the building of new cities and the expansion of old ones.

Nigeria's cities are growing at an ever-increasing rate. Many new residents bring motor vehicles with them, which leads to more exhaust pollution.

A fire is set in the savanna to clear land outside the western town of New Bussa. The demand on Nigeria's cities to expand has meant the loss of sections of savanna and farmland.

Rapid urban growth like this can strain a city's *infrastructure.* For example, a sewage system will become overloaded, raising water pollution levels even further.

There is some hope for the future of Nigeria's environment. In recent years, leaders have been putting stricter antipollution regulations into place. They also have been enforcing existing measures that were formerly over-looked by a corrupt government. It once was common for leaders to receive bribes and kickbacks from industries in exchange for letting environmental requirements go unchecked. And although Nigeria's capital, Abuja, was built in 1976 with an eye toward expansion, it also follows a plan that will most likely anticipate infrastructural problems.

The country's environmental crisis has affected the animal population as well. Large game animals like buffalo and the "big cats"—leopards and lions—have become more rare, and generally are found only in more remote areas and game reserves.

The habitats of Nigeria's monkeys have also suffered. Their tropical rain forests are being destroyed, making it increasingly difficult for the mangabey to find food and shelter. Although exact numbers are hard to come by, conservationists have reported that the mangabey is close to extinction. Sclater's guenon is also losing its home and sources of food, and has been named one of the five most-endangered primates in Africa.

(Opposite) Nigerian students in London celebrate their new independence in the streets, October 1960. After gaining independence from Britain, Nigerians struggled for decades to establish a stable government. (Right) A British-style home in Oshogbo stands as a reminder of the colonists' former role in the country.

2 From Colonialism to Democracy

Beginning in the 19th century, Nigeria's many regional kingdoms were brought under colonial rule. After a long era under the British, Nigeria suffered under military rule before making the eventual transition to the democratically elected government of today. Sometimes these changes were brought about by war; other times, they were made through peaceful negotiation.

There are 250 ethnic groups living in Nigeria today, though during its early history much fewer groups inhabited the land. Historians know little about the earliest identifiable Nigerian culture, known as the Nok, except through its artifacts, found in central Nigeria and dated between 500 B.C. and A.D. 200. Three primary groups appeared later in Nigeria's history: the Hausa-Fulani, the Yoruba, and the Igbo.

The Hausa began establishing kingdoms in the north around A.D. 1000. Although the different Hausa states shared a common language, religion, and culture, each kingdom had its own ruler. They often fought with each other and were *subjugated* by other peoples. In 1804, the Fulanis, led by a Muslim cleric known as Uthman dan Fodio, began a campaign to conquer the Hausa states. They were largely successful, though many Hausa dynasties retreated to the frontier and continued to rule there. Through a series of uprisings started by Muslim revolutionaries like Uthman dan Fodio, the existing states were rooted out and became part of the Sokoto *Caliphate*. By the middle of the 19th century, the new state had extended from the city of Katsina, in the far north, to Ilorin, south of the Niger River, and into present-day Burkina Faso toward the west.

For as long as history can determine, the Yoruba have dominated the area west of the Niger River. They developed strong and complex city-states, the first of which was called Ile-Ife. Their sophisticated organization of government provided people with the freedom and stability to develop their crafts. In particular, they were known for their metal castings and ivory and terra-cotta sculptures, which harken back to the Nok terra-cotta objects that date to 500 B.C. The Yoruba's neighbors, the Edo of Benin, were similarly known for their bronze and brass work. The crafts of these groups became viable sources of trade in West Africa.

Instead of establishing the more common style of monarchy, the Igbo delegated all authority to their self-contained villages. There is a lack of written historical accounts of this group, though historians believe that they formed societies in the eastern region as early as the ninth century

A.D. They were primarily farmers and yams were their main crop. Igbo government was founded on the ideal of a classless society and the principle that all people are equal. Wisdom, decided by age and experience, was the factor by which a leader was deemed fit to govern.

The Slave Trade

By 1500, most of present-day Nigeria was divided into ethnic states. The northern states had become primarily Muslim after Islam spread through West Africa along trans-Saharan trade routes that linked North Africa to the Niger River region. People living in northern Nigeria accepted Islam as early as the 11th century, and the various Islamic states of the West African region, though not directly in control of northern Nigeria, had a profound cultural impact on the people there. By the 16th century, much of the region either paid tribute to the Songhai state, or to Borno, a rival empire.

The Portuguese were the first to capitalize on the trade opportunities that West Africa offered; the Dutch, the French, and the British followed behind them. Between the 15th and mid-19th centuries, the Europeans competed for control of trade along the coast and the rest of southern Nigeria, leaving the northern states generally unhindered. Those states continued to trade heavily in slaves and items like ivory, salt, glass beads, and cloth.

During the years of European expansion and colonization, the Yoruba-ruled southern region of Nigeria was steeped in the slave trade. Civil wars were frequently fought over control of trade. In total, an estimated 3.5 million slaves were shipped from Nigeria to the Americas, where the demand for slave labor was the greatest. Though there were concentrations of Hausa slaves, most were Igbo and Yoruba.

Although the British House of Parliament passed a law in 1807 prohibiting British subjects from participating in the slave trade, European imperialism continued to hold sway over Nigeria. Turning from the system of slavery, the British Empire proceeded to tap other sources of wealth in Nigeria and the surrounding region.

From British Rule to Independence

The new ambition of the British was the manufacture of palm oil, palm kernels, and other goods. They were determined to open up the market by gaining control of the Nigerian coast. In 1862, they annexed Lagos, a thriving port city, after which they gradually expanded their control further along the coast. With the Yoruba wars continually threatening regional security, maintaining coastal control remained an essential goal of the British.

Britain found success by reaching peace settlements with the rulers of rival Yoruba states. In 1893, it established the Oil Rivers Protectorate, which included the Niger Delta, securing control of the trade coming down the Niger River. Between 1901 and 1906, the northern half of Nigeria was brought under British colonial rule, and in 1914 the northern and southern regions were combined to create the Colony and Protectorate of Nigeria. (The name Nigeria, after the Niger River, had been suggested by British journalist Flora Shaw.)

Nigeria was granted self-rule in 1951, and gained its full independence on October 1, 1960. Unlike in other British colonies like Kenya and South

Africa, armed conflict did not bring about this transition. Instead, the British colonial secretary and delegates representing each region of the protectorate reached a peaceful agreement.

The new independent country was led by Governor-General Nnamdi Azikiwe and Abubakar Tafawa Balewa, who had been the prime minister since his appointment in 1957. Nigeria joined the United Nations and became a part of the Commonwealth of Nations, an association of Great Britain, its dependencies, and other affiliated states. The new government was based on a loosely organized federation of self-governing states. When the country became a republic in 1963, Azikiwe was inaugurated as president.

Self-Rule

The people were hopeful about the new republic, but regionalism soon marred the political process. The division of the regions, largely determined by the ethnic groups that populated them, was constantly under dispute. The federal government grew less stable, as many people began to lose faith that it fairly represented the diverse groups of

Great Britain's Duke of Devonshire (left) greets Governor-General Nnamdi Azikiwe, July 1961. Popularly known as "Zik," Azikiwe later served as Nigeria's first president before a coup removed him in 1966.

the country. Military leaders offered a radical solution to the crisis by taking control of the government in 1966, with the republic only three years old. Prime Minister Balewa was assassinated and President Azikiwe was forcibly removed from office. This takeover was followed by a second *coup* later that year, with Colonel Yakubu Gowon claiming power.

Many Nigerians were displeased with Gowon's new government, but only the Igbo minority of the eastern region was moved enough to *secede* from the country. The region was rich in oil, though lacking in other resources, and the Igbo hoped that by removing themselves from the federal system they would no longer have to share their oil wealth. They declared independence from Nigeria on May 30, 1967, calling the new nation the Republic of Biafra. For 31 months, extremely violent civil war claimed about one million civilians and devastated the area. In January 1970, Biafra surrendered to the federal government and rejoined the country.

More military coups occurred in the succeeding years. General Murtala Ramat Muhammad replaced Gowon in a bloodless coup in 1975, and, hoping to restore stability and the people's faith in government, he started a multistage process to establish civilian rule. Assassinated in 1976, he did not complete the transition, though the election of President Alhaji Shehu Shagari in 1979 promised a new beginning.

Although Nigerian oil prices were high and the economy showed promise, civilian rule would not last. The *coalition* that formed the government was weak and there was a lack of cooperation between the party in power and the opposition parties controlling the states. Corruption among government officials was also rampant.

The Biafran War (1967–70), fought over the secession of the oil-rich Eastern Region, was one of the most volatile eras in Nigerian history. These demonstrators at a 1968 rally are calling for a unified country under Head of State Yakubu Gowon.

The military regained power in 1984, marking the beginning of a long period of rotating leadership. Yet another military coup took place in 1985, this time with Major General Ibrahim Babangida assuming power. Civilian rule promised to return in 1993 with an election that showed Chief Moshood Abiola to be the victor. However, only two months after the election, Babangida ruled that the results were inaccurate and reclaimed control.

Shortly after an interim government was instituted, Defense Minister Sani Abacha claimed the presidency.

Democracy was seriously restricted under Abacha's rule. His presidency marred by acts of extreme cruelty and restrictions on human rights, including the imprisonment of Moshood Abiola shortly after the 1993 election (Abiola later died in prison in 1998), and the execution of well-known playwright Ken Saro-Wiwa for anti-government activities. In response to Saro-Wiwa's execution, which was decided after a hasty trial, the Commonwealth suspended Nigeria and the European Union imposed sanctions that remained in place for the rest of Abacha's presidency.

When Abacha died of a heart attack in June 1998, he was replaced by Major General Abdulsalam Abubakar. The people of Nigeria were once again promised the government would return to civilian rule. This time, however, the military leader kept his promise. The winning candidate was Olusegun Obasanjo, a former military leader and political prisoner who was released just eight months before his election. He was sworn in as president in 1999.

Religion and Conflict

The free election of a president could—perhaps should—have meant that Nigeria was on its way to developing the potential that it briefly demonstrated during the early 1980s. The country has remained in a state of conflict, however. Religious and tribal groups have renewed their longstanding hostilities. Since the end of military rule in 1999, it is estimated that more than 10,000 people have been killed in religious conflicts.

A great deal of the civil strife has developed from the enforcement of *Sharia* (Islamic holy law) on Muslims. Sharia is based on the holy book of Islam, the Qur'an (or Koran), and the Sunna, the teachings of the prophet Muhammad. The Sharia prescribes the Islamic way of proper living, covering all areas of life including inheritance, banking, and contract law. Although most of the world's Muslims only adopt certain aspects of Sharia to modify their personal conduct, in northern Nigeria and several Middle Eastern countries it has been instituted as criminal law. In the states in which Sharia has this level of authority, perpetrators may receive severe punishments. For example, women convicted of improper sexual practices may be lashed or even stoned to death; apprehended thieves may have their hands amputated.

The estimated 50 percent of Nigerians who are Muslim embrace Islamic law. Islamic leaders argue that because Sharia is not enforced for Christians and people who practice traditional religions, it has a legitimate place in the religious courts and should not be repealed. Nonetheless, the minority of Christians living in the north, along with the southern non-Muslims who trade in the northern cities of Kano and Kaduna, believe that Sharia violates people's basic rights.

One major event that resulted from the Sharia controversy was the Kaduna riots of November 2002. Abuja was the intended site of the annual Miss World beauty pageant, scheduled for the following month, but Muslims living in the Kaduna region thought that the competition was improper and violated religious code. The riots they initiated lasted for four days and claimed the lives of more than 200 people.

A Nigerian reads about the riots that took place in the northern city of Kaduna in November 2002. Over 200 people died in the civil unrest, which broke out over the decision to make Abuja the intended site of the Miss World beauty pageant. The competition was considered offensive by many of the country's Muslims.

Ethnicity is often an additional point of conflict, as was the case in the clashes between the northern Islamic Hausas and the mainly Christian Yorubas of the southwest in February 2002. About 100 people were killed in the fighting in Lagos.

Looking Ahead

During the 1970s, Nigeria had the 33rd-highest per capita income in the world, and by the early 1980s, the country was heralded for its prosperity. However, after those successful years the economy suffered tremendously, and by 1997 the per capita income had dropped to become the 13th lowest in the world. This was largely the result of many years of government corruption, the burden of external debt, and the pressure placed on the government to increase domestic spending.

The hopes that many Nigerians had with the 1999 election of President Obasanjo have since been muted. Although he had promised to stop corruption and financial mismanagement, one of his projects was planning the construction of a soccer stadium that cost $330 million—more than the country's budget for health care and education combined.

Following a first term that disappointed many people, Olusegun Obasanjo was elected to a second term in April 2003 with over 60 percent of the vote. Opposition parties and international election observers claimed that election fraud had taken place, but Obasanjo remained in office.

(Opposite) A woman casts her vote at a booth in Lagos. In recent years, a civilian government has monitored elections instead of the military. Many people are participating in the transition to civilian rule. (Right) Nigerian tribal chiefs attend the 2003 Commonwealth Heads of Government Meeting, a summit for leaders of Nigeria, Great Britain, and other states.

3 Governing Nigeria Today

AFTER SPENDING MOST of the post-independence years under military rule, Nigerians are striving to make the transition to civilian rule. In 1999, two events signaled the advent of a new era—the election of President Obasanjo and the adoption of a new constitution.

The Constitution

There are many similarities between the new Nigerian constitution and the U.S. Constitution. For example, like the U.S. government, Nigeria's government is now divided into three branches—executive, legislative, and judicial. The Nigerian constitution establishes the positions that comprise each branch, as well as the responsibilities of each branch and the rights and duties of the citizens.

The list of the rights granted to Nigerian citizens is extensive. Many of the listed rights sound similar to those found in the U.S. Constitution's Bill of Rights, such as the right to a fair hearing, to freedom of expression, and to peaceful assembly and association, though there are others not explicitly stated in the American document. These include the rights to freedom of movement within Nigeria and to live wherever one chooses, the right to life, and the right to private and family life (in other words, a person's mail, telephone conversations, and homes are guaranteed to be private). The Nigerian constitution places great importance on personal dignity, with provisions for the right to dignity of human persons as well as the right to freedom from discrimination.

The powers, duties, and responsibilities of the individual states are also included in the Nigerian constitution. The state governments are made up of the same branches as the federal government, with the exception that states do not have a senate but only a house of assembly. The executive branch consists of the governor and the deputy governor. States also have a high court and a court of appeal, as well as courts to handle cases that fall under Sharia law.

The constitution also establishes the structure and nature of Nigeria's political parties. In order to prevent parties from arbitrarily receiving too much power—as has happened in the past—strict guidelines have been created. Sections of the constitution spell out clearly how a political party should be formed, who may join it, and how it should raise and spend funds.

Finally, the constitution calls for universal suffrage for Nigerians. Everyone 18 years of age and older can vote. The president is elected by popular vote, and he or she cannot serve more than two terms, each four years long. Because of Nigeria's history of election fraud and political misconduct, international observers were sent to observe the presidential elections of 1999 and 2003. Although there was a consensus that fraud occurred, observers also agreed that it did not greatly affect the outcome of the election. As of this writing, Olusegun Obasanjo is serving his second presidential term; the next election is scheduled for May 2007.

The Executive Branch

The executive branch consists of the president, vice president, and the cabinet. The president serves as the chief of state, the head of government, and the commander-in-chief of Nigeria's armed forces. As chief of state, the president has the final approval over most decisions, including making judicial appointments and signing or vetoing new legislation. As commander-in-chief, the president oversees how the armed forces are staffed, trained, equipped, and deployed. In general, he or she oversees the daily activities of the government and is the one who must, in the end, accept much of the blame for its mistakes.

The Federal Executive Council acts as the cabinet of the Nigerian government. There are 28 cabinet ministers who are appointed to oversee specific ministries, which include Agriculture, Communications, Defense, Education and Youth Development, Environment, Foreign Affairs, Health and Social Services, Industries, and Petroleum Resources.

The Legislative Branch

The *bicameral* National Assembly is made up of the Senate and the House of Assembly. There are 107 seats in the Senate—three from each state and one from the Federal Capital Territory, Abuja—and 346 members of the House of

The president of Nigeria, Olusegun Obasanjo (left), attends a summit with President Abdoulaye Wade of Senegal (center) and President Yoweri Museveni of Uganda, April 2004. As leader of a newly formed civilian government, Obasanjo faces the challenge of preserving democracy.

Assembly. Members of both the House and the Senate are elected to four-year terms by popular vote and must sit for a minimum of 181 days each year.

The National Assembly functions in much the same way as the U.S. Congress. Both government bodies are responsible for exposing fraud and corruption. Most importantly, they make laws that help the government function efficiently and fairly. The bills created by the National Assembly can potentially become the laws that govern aspects of citizens' lives. Each house has several specialized committees that focus on areas of national life. Such committees include Aviation, Ethics, Petroleum, and Police Affairs.

Either the Senate or the House can introduce a bill. If the other governing body also passes the bill, it is sent to the president who can sign it or withhold his or her signature. If the president does not approve the bill, it can still become a law if a two-thirds majority of the Senate and House pass the bill.

All members of the Assembly serve identical terms, meaning that all seats are up for election at the same time—four years from the date that the House first met. To become a member of the Senate, one must be a citizen of Nigeria and be at least 35 years old. The House also requires Nigerian citizenship and that the member be at least 30 years of age.

The Judicial Branch

Nigerian law is based primarily on English common law and tradition. There are three major federal courts: the Supreme Court, Court of Appeals, and High Court.

U.S. president Bill Clinton addresses the Nigerian National Assembly during his official visit in August 2000. The National Assembly, made up of a Senate and House of Assembly, operates much like the U.S. Congress.

The president appoints the judges to the Supreme Court, made up of the Chief Justice and a maximum of 21 judges—the exact number of judges is set by the National Assembly. The appointments are made with the recommendation of the National Judicial Council and the approval of the Senate.

The Court of Appeals listens to cases that have been already ruled in lower courts and now face appeal. It is comprised of the court's president and a maximum of 49 justices. The president and the justices are appointed by Nigeria's president, with the recommendation of the National Judicial Council and the final approval of the Senate.

The High Court handles civil cases that involve such matters as taxes, customs and duties, and important contract disputes. As with the heads of the other courts, the Chief Judge is also president-appointed and confirmed by the Senate. The constitution does not set down the official number of High Court judges; instead, the National Assembly makes that decision.

Due to the strong influence of Islamic law, the constitution has made allowances for Sharia. On the state level, there are courts that handle disputes under Sharia law. There is also a Sharia Court of Appeal in the Federal Capital Territory, Abuja. To ensure that the Court of Appeals can make fair rulings on Sharia, no fewer than three of its members must be versed in Islamic personal law.

Political Parties

As of this writing, the Nigeria's major parties are the ruling People's Democratic Party (PDP) and the leading opposition group, the All Nigeria Peoples' Party (ANPP). Other important opposition parties are the United

Nigeria People's Party (UNPP) and the All Progressive Grand Alliance (APGA).

As in the United States, the composition of political parties and their missions vary. The PDP, which is the affiliation of President Olusegun Obasanjo, is a coalition made up of veteran politicians and several retired generals. One of the continuing missions of the PDP is to make certain that the voters can always elect candidates of their own choosing. The ANPP is the second-largest political party in Nigeria and is a relatively new group. It is a conservative organization made up of wealthy businesspeople and politicians. One of the ANPP's stated goals is to facilitate and promote a peaceful coexistence among Nigerians, in spite of their varied ethnic and cultural backgrounds.

Charges of election fraud have plagued Nigeria's political process in recent years. Following President Obasanjo's sweep of the votes in the 2003 election, Chairman of the All Nigeria Peoples Party Don Etiebet (center) and other opposition leaders made accusations of foul play.

Although nearly three-quarters of Nigerians are employed in the agricultural sector, producing food for the rapidly growing population remains difficult. (Opposite) A worker washes rice in Makurdi. (Right) Girls sell peanuts on a street in Kaduna.

4 An Economy in Need of Reform

BECAUSE NIGERIA IS rich in oil, many people mistakingly think it is a prosperous nation. However, the economy has suffered from years of corruption and mismanagement. Today, Nigeria is evolving as it adapts to a new civilian government and its economy undergoes major reforms.

In addition to oil and oil products, Nigeria's industries process tin, palm oil, peanuts, rubber, textiles, and chemicals. The country's major exports are the products from these industries, and its primary trading partners are the United States, Brazil, Spain, Indonesia, France, and India.

Oil

Oil and oil products have been the greatest source of revenue throughout much of Nigeria's history. Nigeria is one of the largest exporters of oil in the world and is a member of the Organization of Petroleum Exporting

Quick Facts: The Economy of Nigeria

Gross domestic product (GDP*):
$112.5 billion
Inflation: 14.2%
Natural resources: natural gas, petroleum, tin, columbite, iron ore, coal, limestone, lead, zinc, arable land
Agriculture (45% of GDP): cocoa, peanuts, palm oil, corn, rice, sorghum, millet, cassava (tapioca), yams, rubber, cattle, sheep, goats, pigs, timber, fish
Industry (20% of GDP): crude oil, coal, tin, columbine, palm oil, peanuts, cotton, rubber, wood, hides and skins, textiles, cement and other construction materials, food products, footwear, chemicals, fertilizer, printing, ceramics, steel
Services (35% of GDP): government, other

Foreign Trade:
Exports—$17.3 billion: petroleum and petroleum products 95%, cocoa, rubber
Imports—$13.6 billion: machinery, chemicals, transport equipment, manufactured goods, food and live animals
Economic growth rate: 3.2%
Currency exchange rate: U.S. $1 = 134.95 Nigerian nairas (2004)

*GDP is the total value of goods and services produced in a country annually.
All figures are 2002 estimates unless otherwise indicated.
Sources: CIA World Factbook, 2003; Bloomberg.com.

Countries (OPEC). In 2002, it was the fifth-largest supplier of crude oil to the United States. During the years of Nigeria's military rule, oil was so plentiful that leaders failed to look after its other industries.

Much of Nigeria's oil production is through joint business ventures with companies such as Shell, ChevronTexaco, and ExxonMobil. Though some reserves have been found offshore, most of the country's oil comes from the region along the Niger River Delta. However, with violence, labor strikes, and crime often suspending production in the area, the multinational companies face certain risks by conducting business in the area.

Although oil brings in a great deal of wealth, the general population of Nigeria does not benefit directly from the oil industry. The unemployment rate was reported by the country's Federal Office of Statistics to be over 40 percent in late 2002. According to other 2002 estimates, 60 percent of the Nigerian population fell below the poverty line, and the *gross national income per capita* was $290 in 2003.

One reason why the people do not directly benefit from the oil industry is that it requires a great deal

In recent years, an organized force of Nigerian oil workers has continually made demands for better treatment in the workplace, with only modest results. Organized protests, like this one held in Lagos in May 2003, are commonplace, and strikes often stop production at oil plants.

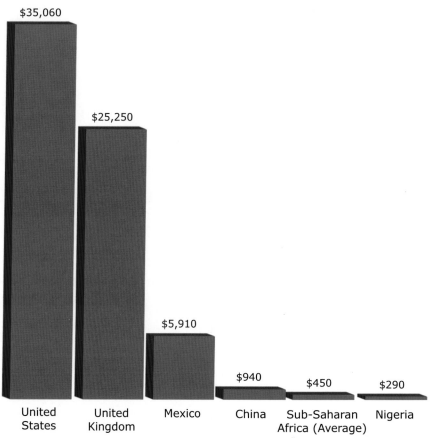

Gross National Income (GNI) Per Capita of Nigeria and Other Countries*

United States	$35,060
United Kingdom	$25,250
Mexico	$5,910
China	$940
Sub-Saharan Africa (Average)	$450
Nigeria	$290

*Gross national income per capita is the total value of all goods and services produced domestically in a year, supplemented by income received from abroad, divided by midyear population. The above figures take into account fluctuations in currency exchange rates and differences in inflation rates across global economies.

All figures are 2002 estimates. Source: World Bank, 2003.

of the country's *capital resources.* As a result, these resources are not available for the development of additional industries or for providing aid in areas where agriculture is still the primary source of income.

As the oil industry has grown, environmental challenges have also developed. Oil spills, deforestation, and gas flaring have long been problems associated with the industry. The military governments of the past closed their eyes to the problems and were lax with air and water pollution regulations. Under the present civilian rule, officials are more consistently enforcing regulations. They are also putting more regulations in place to help curtail the damage. Large cities are promoting the use of alternative, renewable energy sources like fuel wood to limit the air pollution caused by the increasing numbers of motor vehicles.

Agriculture

Nigeria's primary agricultural crops are cocoa, peanuts, palm oil, rice, cassava (manioc or tapioca), and livestock, which include cattle, sheep, goats, and pigs. Until oil was discovered, the foundation of Nigeria's economy was the *subsistence farming* sector. The country relied on crops and livestock for its food and income. With the development of the oil industry, the agricultural sector has received less and less attention over the years. Droughts in the north and a shortage of fertilizer in 1996 have added to farmers' continuing struggles. Today, many young people are leaving behind the land that their families have farmed for generations—and the agricultural industry completely—for the cities to search for more financially rewarding jobs.

Although an estimated 70 percent of Nigerians are employed in the agricultural sector, farming has not been able to meet the needs of a rapidly growing population. And although approximately 31 percent of the land is suitable for crops, only about 3 percent is being farmed. The country has not been agriculturally self-sufficient since the 1970s. Once a major exporter of food, it now must import a great deal in order to feed its people.

To help with the shortage of agricultural revenue, and to move Nigeria away from its dependence on the oil industry, the government has offered export subsidies to farmers. However, until farm equipment is modernized and roads are improved to facilitate transport, the country will not reach its potential in this field.

Tourism

Political and ethnic unrest, carjackings, thefts, kidnappings, murders. Reports of these crimes and events don't find their way into many tourist brochures, nor are they the kinds of events that draw visitors to a country. Because they have been very common in many parts of Nigeria, the tourist industry has struggled and contributed only minimally to the national economy.

Although the U.S. State Department still issues travel advisories and warnings, Nigeria has made attempts to improve tourists' safety. The adventurous traveler who can look past the warnings finds a diverse culture and spectacular natural attractions. There are caves, rock formations including the Chukuku Hills, the Agwai Hills, Riyom Rock, and the Zuma rocks, waterfalls in southwest and central Nigeria, the Jos Plateau, and other sites for those eager to seek them out. If more people were to visit

Nigeria, the tourist business could expand and help the country become less dependent on its petroleum ventures. That can not happen, however, while violence is still widespread.

Strengthening the Economy

When the economic boom of the early 1980s proved to be short-lived, Nigeria was left in a desperate situation. The many years of military rule and corruption had injured the economy. The escalating rate of HIV/AIDS cases also incapacitated many workers living in their 20s and 30s, when they are the most economically productive. It had also become difficult to meet the demands of a population that was increasing rapidly, the result of a high birth rate and a constant influx of people fleeing crises in neighboring countries. Yet another cause of Nigeria's economic struggles was the increasing foreign debt—by 2000 it was estimated to be over $34 billion. Rather than seeing an end to the debt, forecasts only anticipated deepening poverty. Nigeria needed help.

In 2000, Nigeria received a $1-billion credit from the International Monetary Fund (IMF), payable as long as specific economic reforms—such as the reduction of large wage demands and the resolution of regional disputes—were made within a set period of time. This agreement expired, however, and Nigeria received less financial help than expected in 2002. During the recent transition from military to civilian rule, Nigeria has been hard pressed to put these reforms into place.

It is clear that the country cannot rely on international aid to pull it out of debt without further developing its industrial and agricultural sectors. To reach this goal, the present government has offered tax credit incentives to domestic

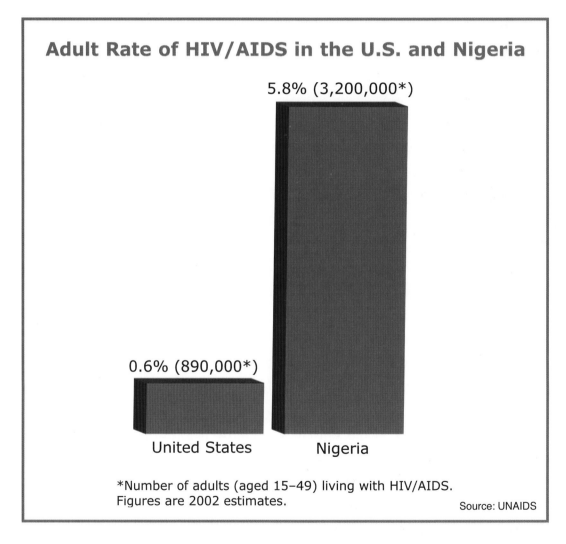

Adult Rate of HIV/AIDS in the U.S. and Nigeria

5.8% (3,200,000*)

0.6% (890,000*)

United States   Nigeria

*Number of adults (aged 15–49) living with HIV/AIDS.
Figures are 2002 estimates.

Source: UNAIDS

businesses. These include tax credits for any industry using local resources and production methods that require more than 1,000 employees, as well as a tax deduction of up to 120 percent for research and development expenses.

The Nigerian government has also implemented measures to help protect businesses from foreign competition. It has placed limitations on importing items that domestic industries are able to produce on their own. The most recent additions to the list of banned items include textiles, men's footwear, soaps and detergents, furniture, assembled bicycles, flowers (real and artificial), small farm equipment, and corrugated boards and cartons.

No matter what measures are put into place, repairing the Nigerian economy will not be easy or quick—especially with an ever-increasing population, a neglected infrastructure, and an oil industry that has yet to reach its production potential.

(Opposite) A student reads from the Qur'an in an Islamic school in northern Nigeria. The low levels of literacy and school enrollment are major sources of concern. Many families keep their children out of schools so that they may work at home. (Right) A mother lets her child sleep comfortably as she sifts grain.

5 Nigeria's Culture and People

IF ONLY ONE word could be used to describe Nigeria's culture and people, it would have to be *diverse*. After all, what could one expect from a country that has 250 ethnic groups that speak 505 languages!

Nigeria's ethnicity derives from its tribal roots. The largest groups today are the Hausa and Fulani, Yoruba, Igbo, and Ijaw. English is the official language, though the languages of these groups are spoken in the regions in which they have settled.

Education

Education is compulsory for children between the ages of six and twelve, though few study beyond those years. There are three school levels: primary, secondary, and tertiary. Children must be at least six years old to

Quick Facts: The People of Nigeria

Population: 133,881,703

Ethnic groups: Nigeria, which is Africa's most populous country, is composed of more than 250 ethnic groups; the following are the most populous and politically influential: Hausa and Fulani 29%, Yoruba 21%, Igbo (Ibo) 18%, Ijaw 10%, Kanuri 4%, Ibibio 3.5%, Tiv 2.5%

Age structure:
0–14 years: 43.6%
15–64 years: 53.6%
65 years and over: 2.8%

Population growth rate: 2.53%

Birth rate: 38.75 births/1,000 population

Infant mortality rate: 71.35 deaths/1,000 live births

Death rate: 13.76 deaths/ 1,000 population

Life expectancy at birth:
total population: 51.01 years
male: 50.89 years
female: 51.14 years

Total fertility rate: 5.4 children born/woman

Religions: Muslim 50%, Christian 40%, indigenous beliefs 10%

Languages: English (official), Hausa, Yoruba, Igbo (Ibo), Fulani

Literacy: 68%

All figures are 2003 estimates unless indicated.
Source: Adapted from CIA World Factbook, 2003.

enter primary school, at which they spend a maximum of six years. Secondary school is divided into junior secondary and senior secondary, each of which is attended for three years. After passing a college entrance test, a student may attend university.

The literacy rate in Nigeria is low—an estimated 68 percent. Despite the government's attempts to improve the educational system by making primary school education compulsory, the United Nations Children's Fund (UNICEF) estimated in 1999 that approximately 4 million children, most of whom lived in villages, did not have access to education. Those who were receiving an education typically went to schools that were run-down and lacked basic equipment, or were instructed by teachers who were not properly trained. In 2001, it was estimated that approximately 23 percent of Nigeria's teachers did not have the required minimum certification to teach.

Despite the low performance levels of primary and secondary schools, enrollment is expanding at the university level. Between 1980 and 2002, it was estimated that the number of university students had increased from 55,000 to 400,000.

The University of Ibadan is one of the country's most reputable universities, thanks in part to its renowned teaching hospital. In recent decades, enrollment at Nigeria's universities has risen.

Religion

Generally, religion is an important part of everyday life for Nigerians, of whom 50 percent are Muslim and 40 percent are Christian. The remaining 10 percent practice indigenous religions usually specific to their particular ethnic group. In most cases, groups worship their own set of spirits or gods and goddesses acknowledged as the world's creators. Some groups believe that spirits watch over different aspects of community life, or are a guiding force in crop growth, rainfall, and other natural phenomena. Figurines like the *ibeji* (twin dolls with beads) are very popular among indigenous groups and are worn as good-luck charms.

Although the Nigerian constitution guarantees freedom of religion, there are still conflicts that have emerged concerning religious practice. The most prevalent of these is the Muslim-Christian conflict surrounding the expansion of Sharia law into the southern states. In the northern part of Nigeria, where Islam remains the major religion, Sharia law has long been in effect in the domestic and civil spheres. However, the Christians who make up the southern states have opposed the expansion into the region, which threatens to implement two separate sets of laws.

Disputes over the expansion of Sharia law have resulted in the deaths of hundreds of Nigerians. When many of the northern states decided to enforce Sharia law for criminal offenses in 2000, more than 1,000 people were killed in the ensuing riots between Christians and Muslims. As some communities in the southern states have expressed a desire to follow Sharia law, the violence has continued. The extreme punishments of Sharia law, which include stoning and mutilation, are of great concern to the growing population of Christians. They are also troubled that women receive a disproportionate number of the sentences.

Art

Nigeria's art forms are as diverse as its population. The earliest *excavated* art objects, dating back as early as 500 B.C., were made through iron smelt-

Two Muslim men hold a discussion in front of the Katsina Sharia Court of Appeal, where death sentences may be decided for those convicted of breaking *Sharia* (Islamic) law. The enforcement of Sharia law, most common in the north, has always been one of the most heated issues for the religiously diverse populace.

ing and are products of the Nok culture. Some of the more well-known art works of later periods are attributed to the Benin and the Yoruba. Benin artifacts are made of bronze and copper. Yoruba masks, some of which can be seen at major museums, are wood-carved and represent the forces of nature and the gods. They are still used in traditional ceremonies today, such as the Gelede masquerade and funerals (the masks are believed to quiet the spirits

Nigerian artists are known for such crafts as grass weaving, wood-carving, leatherwork, and pottery. Here a merchant in the northern city of Kano sells calabashes, hollowed-out shells used as containers.

of the deceased). The Yoruba also have made terra-cotta and ivory sculptures that are familiar to collectors throughout the world.

Art forms that can be found in Nigeria today include painting, grass weaving, wood-carving, ivory carving, glass and metal work, pottery, cloth weaving, and leatherwork. As in the past, today's Nigerian artists take advantage of the materials that are readily available to them. For example, many craftspeople living in the north use the plentiful grass there to make beautifully designed and practical objects like sturdy baskets and durable floor mats.

Music

As can be expected, the music of Nigeria is greatly influenced by the traditions of the country's ethnic groups, yet Nigerian musicians are also not immune to foreign influences. Seal, the son of a Nigerian, and the Nigerian-born Sade are two internationally known singers who have found success with other styles of music.

Juju is a popular native form of music and probably the best-known genre outside of Nigeria. It evolved from the palm wine music of the 1920s and 1930s. During those years, it was common for eastern Nigerian guitarists and drummers to play at parties where people drank palm wine. The *genre* named after the wine emerged from the mixture of local melodies and rhythms and Trinidadian calypso.

Lagos is known as the birthplace of Fuji music, which features western Nigerian vocals and percussion instruments. It shares many characteristics with Islamic music and is often played at religious ceremonies. Panko, a widely popular and upbeat style, is based on the lively dance rhythms of eastern Nigeria.

Traditional musicians perform at the Argungu Fishing Festival, held every year in Kebbi State. Nigerian styles of music have been influenced by various foreign genres, including Islamic and Caribbean music.

Cuisine

Nigerian cooks use many of the same meat ingredients that North American cooks use—beef, chicken, turkey, shrimp, crab, and other types of seafood, though they use different spices and yams that serve as the base for various meals. Also, Nigerian cooks often use other foods—goat, geese, guinea fowl, or pigeon—that are not as likely to appear on a North American dinner table.

Nigeria's tropical location provides tropical fruits such as bananas, pineapples, and limes. Other common fruits are oranges, tangerines, watermelon and other melons, guava, mangoes, and apples. The apples are not like the ones found in Western hemisphere, but are smaller and pink and white.

Most of the vegetables that are popular in North America are also used in Nigerian cooking. Palm oil, made from the palm kernel, is the most common cooking agent. Because they are plentiful, grains and beef are common ingredients, particularly in the northern states. Grains such as millet, corn rice, and maize play a major role in the Nigerian diet, and popular snack foods include fried yam chips, fried *plantains*, and meat pies.

The expansion of Lagos and other Nigerian cities has had both positive and negative results. (Opposite) A slum lies next to a major highway in Lagos. (Right) A crowded market, located near a bus station, is alive with traders and shoppers.

6 The Cities

MOST OF NIGERIA'S nearly 134 million residents live in rural areas. However, the growth of the national population has bolstered significant growth in the major cities, which include Kano, Lagos, Ibadan, and the new capital city of Abuja. Like other expanding cities of Africa, these cities deal with many pressing problems, such as overcrowding, homelessness, and pollution.

Abuja

In 1976, the Nigerian federal government decided to begin moving the capital from Lagos to Abuja and to establish the surrounding region as the Federal Capital Territory. The area was inhabited by an ethnic group known as the Gwari, who had to be removed from their land to make room for the new capital. Most government operations moved to Abuja in 1991.

Several factors went into the decision to move the capital to Abuja; the

59

most obvious of these were the city's prime location, moderate climate, and available space for growth. Abuja is situated in the geographic center of the country, making it accessible from other regions. It is also conveniently bordered to the north by the convergence of the Niger and Benue Rivers. Because of the surrounding area's low population density, there is room for the city to expand.

The greater *metropolitan* area covers 3,089 square miles (8,000 sq km), while the actual city area is only 96.5 square miles (250 sq km). Built in the 1980s, it is the first Nigerian city whose expansion has been closely anticipated, though its population is still small, estimated at 171,800 in 2004. Abuja's high-rise buildings, shopping facilities, nightclubs, and modern international hotels are surrounded by impressive natural features, including the Chukuku Hills, the Agwai Hills, and the Zuma rocks. Scattered throughout these formations are popular tourist sites and mountain climbing destinations.

Lagos

With an estimated population of 8,682,200 in 2004, Lagos is the largest city in Nigeria and one of the second largest in Africa, next to Cairo. It covers approximately 116 square miles (300 sq km) and is located on a group of islands. Until 1991, Lagos was Nigeria's national capital. It was settled in the 15th century by the Yoruba, and after serving as a fishing and farming settlement, was a trading post for the Portuguese until the British traders arrived in the 1800s.

In 1862, the British declared Lagos a colony. It remained under British control until Nigeria gained its independence in 1960. Seven years later the Biafran war broke out (1967–70), after which there was a large migration to the city that created a population boom. Today, Lagos is of the world's five largest cities, and it is still growing.

Immediately after Nigerian independence, Lagos became a center of light industry. With the development of the oil industry, however, business leaders in Lagos switched their focus to oil products, which left the city vulnerable to the fluctuating international oil market. The infrastructure could not keep up with the city's growing population, and there was a shortage of clean water. Along with not providing drinking water, the neighboring Gulf of Guinea and the creeks that ran through the city caused frequent flooding.

With the rapidly increasing population, there was also a lack of affordable and available housing, making slums a common phenomenon. When the economy slowed in the late 1970s and early 1980s, programs to improve the infrastructure had to be abandoned. However, since 1985, city leaders have made major attempts to improve conditions in Lagos, with plans to build new sewers and drainage systems.

Along with being the commercial hub and industrial center of Nigeria, Lagos is known for its nightclubs and live music. Since the city is extremely crowded, traffic is a serious problem. In the most congested sections it can take an average of between two and three hours to travel 6 to 12 miles (10–20 km).

Tourist attractions include the National Theater, the palace of Oba (Lagos' traditional leader), and beaches along the Gulf of Guinea. The National Museum, on Lagos Island, is home to bronze sculptures and ivory carvings from Benin, as well as masks and terra-cotta sculptures from the city of Jos. It also has on display the bullet-riddled car in which former president Murtala Muhammad was assassinated in 1976.

Kano

Kano, the second-largest city in Nigeria and the largest city in the north, had an estimated population of 3,412,900 in 2004. It is located in northwest Nigeria, approximately 520 miles (835 km) from Lagos. Over 1,000 years old, Kano is the oldest major city in *sub-Saharan* Africa.

Kano was one of the seven city-states established by the Hausa. Its written history can be traced to A.D. 999, but it is believed that the city was already several hundred years old by that time. In 1809, the Fulani captured Kano, by that time a thriving commercial and trading center thanks to its precious dyed cloth. The British took the city in 1903, and it became part of the Northern Nigerian British Protectorate until the country's independence.

Kano remains a major commercial and industrial center, with dyed cloth a main commodity. Other important exports are hides, animal skins, and peanuts, which are also bagged and stored for shipment to Lagos. Kano is also one of Nigeria's educational centers. It contains Bayero University and Kano State Institute for Higher Education, as well as the headquarters of the British Council Library.

Cyclists pass through the ancient gate of Kano, part of a Hausa fortress built in the 15th century. Other sections of the mud wall, which was once 11 miles (16 km) in circumference, are also still standing.

One of the impressive features of this Muslim city is the surrounding mud wall. Reportedly built in the 15th century, the wall was once 11 miles (18 km) in circumference and had 16 gates. Today, in the area known as the Old City, the gates remain though the wall has mostly disintegrated. The main gate, the Kofar Mata Gate, leads to the emir's palace and the central mosque. No one is allowed in the palace without an official invitation, and the mosque is only open to Muslims. Built in the 15th century, Gidan Makama Museum draws a lot of visitors with its extensive historical collection covering Kano and the Hausa and Fulani peoples.

Ibadan

Ibadan, located in southwest Nigeria, is the country's third-largest city, with a population of roughly 3,201,500 in 2004. The capital of the state of Oyo, Ibadan is located at the edge of the forest belt. It was originally named Eba-Odan after a nearby town.

The city was founded in the 1830s to serve as a military camp during the Yoruba civil wars. It went on to become a powerful Yoruba city-state. In 1893, Ibadan became part of the British protectorate, as well as the capital of Nigeria's former Western Region.

Besides being the state capital, Ibadan is a commercial center, producing metal products, furniture, and soap and trading cotton that is picked in the region. It is also home to one of Nigeria's most prestigious schools, the University of Ibadan, and its teaching hospital. Many visitors to the city journey to the historic towns outside the city, such as Ogbomosho, Ijebu-Ode, and Oshogbo.

The rooftops of Ibadan, located in southwest Nigeria. Once a powerful Yoruba city-state, Ibadan is a thriving commercial center today.

Kaduna

The fourth-largest city in Nigeria is Kaduna, with a 2004 population estimated at 1,563,300. Located on the Kaduna River in northwest Nigeria, Kaduna was founded by the British in 1913. In 1917, it became the capital of Nigeria's Northern Region, which it remained until 1967.

Kaduna is an important transportation hub, with roads going in five directions from the city. The easy access into the city helps make it an important communications and industrial center as well. Its major industries are cotton-textiles, beverages, and furniture manufacturing.

The National Museum in Kaduna has an impressive collection of historical art and artifacts. Its major displays include wood-carvings, masks, Nok terra-cotta figures, and Benin bronzes.

Other Communities

Port Harcourt is the fifth-largest city in Nigeria (estimated 2004 population: 1,133,000). Located on the Bonny River in the southeast part of the country, it is the capital of Rivers State, and was established by the British in 1913. It was named after Lewis, Viscount Harcourt, who was the secretary of state for the British colonies from 1910 until 1915.

The country's oil industry is centered in Port Harcourt. It is also a major manufacturing center, producing steel, aluminum products, tires, paint, footwear, bicycles, and motor vehicles.

Although not one of Nigeria's largest cities, Ile-Ife (pronounced *EE-lay EE-fay*, which means "old city") has garnered a reputation for its heritage of Yoruba culture. The city is located in southwest Nigeria, in the state of Osun, approximately 40 miles (64 km) west of Ibadan.

Early on, Ile-Ife (also called Ife) became an important center for Yoruba sculpture. Many of the terra-cotta figures and bronzes that are seen in the city today date from the 12th to 15th centuries. In many cases, these items were crafted and given to the *oni*, or king, as a **tithe.**

Ile-Ife was officially founded by the Yoruba in A.D. 1300. According to Yoruba **mythology,** the city sits on the land where the group's civilization began. Oduduwa, the creator of the earth, founded the city of Ile-Ife. Upon descending from the skies and finding only water, he emptied a container of soil from which a town could spring up. He then sent his sons, who were priest-kings, to rule over the other Yoruba cities.

A Calendar of Nigerian Festivals

Local festivals in Nigeria predate the establishment of major religions and continue to be practiced. Dancing and masquerades are usually the highlight of the festivals. Performances are often given by professional dance troupes that travel from village to village. Festivals may celebrate harvests, weddings, installations of new chiefs, and even funerals. Rather than being an occasion of sadness, the death of a loved one is seen as a return of that person to ancestors who have already died.

Many of the festivals do not have fixed dates on the calendar, such as the **Eyo Festival**, which is held in Lagos. Although the festival can be held anytime, it is usually reserved as part of the final burial rights for a highly regarded chief. The festival pays homage to the *oba* (leader) of Lagos. The main highway is closed, and an elaborate procession is held. Other festivals without fixed dates celebrate the harvest and other natural events.

January

Many Nigerians celebrate **New Year's Day**. As in many other countries, the day is celebrated with parties, feasting, and fireworks.

February/March

At the end of the growing season, Nigerians celebrate the harvest by holding the **Argungu Fishing Festival** along the Argungu River near Sokoto. Men and boys have 45 minutes to enter the river and try to catch as many fish as they can with a net. This fishing derby is followed by activities like canoe racing, wild duck hunting, diving competitions, and singing and dancing.

May

May 1 is **Worker's Day**, a day that celebrates workers in Nigeria. Laborers rally across the country and union members listen to speeches.

July

The **Yoruba Oro Festival** (also called the **Bullroarer Festival**) lasts several nights and is held in July. The men put on masks and walk the streets while the women remain inside and out of sight, because according to Oro cult belief, a woman could die just by seeing one of the masqueraders.

August

One of the biggest Igbo festivals is the **New Yam Festival (Iri-ji)**, which comes at the end of one work cycle and signals the beginning of a new one. The Igbo believe that a new cycle must begin with only new yams. Thus, on the night before the festival, all of the old yams are thrown out; the new yams are offered first to the gods and ancestors and then to the villagers.

October

October 1 is **National Day**, also known as **Independence Day**. People commemorate Nigeria's independence from the British in 1960. Students and workers have the day off to attend parades and special ceremonies.

66

A Calendar of Nigerian Festivals

November

The Kalabari people of Rivers State celebrate the **Akaso Festival** every two years. The festival begins around the third Thursday in November and lasts for four days. It is a time for thanking the goddess Akaso for her protection and to cleanse the people from any evil.

The **Sharo/Shadi Festival** is usually held after the rainy season. Unmarried men from the Fulani towns of Katsina, Kano, and Adamawa voluntarily face the whippings of fellow townspeople to prove their strength and courage.

December

Boxing Day, held on December 26, is a festival that originated in Great Britain. The traditional custom on this day is to give presents to the less fortunate. Many Nigerians also go to beaches and have picnics.

Religious Observances

Nigerian Muslims and Christians observe a number of important holy days related to their religions. Some of these are on particular days each year (for example, **Christmas**, which is observed on December 25, is the Christian celebration of the birth of Jesus). However, many other major celebrations are held according to a lunar calendar, in which the months are related to the phases of the moon. A lunar month is shorter than the typical month of the Western calendar. Therefore, the festival dates vary from year to year. Other celebrations are observed seasonally.

A very important month of the Muslim lunar calendar is the ninth month, **Ramadan**. This is a time of sacrifice for devout Muslims. Nigerian Muslims celebrate **Eid al-Fitr** to mark the end of Ramadan. The festival begins with prayers and is followed by drumming and other forms of entertainment.

Eid al-Adha (Feast of Sacrifice) takes place in the last month of the Muslim calendar during the hajj period, when Muslims make a pilgrimage to Mecca. The holiday honors the prophet Abraham, who was willing to sacrifice his own son to Allah. Each of these holidays is celebrated with a feast. On Eid al-Adha, families traditionally eat a third of the feast and donate the rest to the poor. **Eid al-Maulud**, usually taking place sometime around September, celebrates the birth of Muhammad around A.D. 570. It is a customary time for those with money to give to the poor.

The major Christian festivals on the lunar cycle involve the suffering and death of Jesus Christ. **Ash Wednesday** marks the start of a period of self-sacrifice called **Lent**, which lasts for 40 days. The final eight days of Lent are known as **Holy Week**. A number of important days are observed, including **Palm Sunday**, which commemorates Jesus' arrival in Jerusalem; **Holy Thursday**, which marks the night of the Last Supper; **Good Friday**, the day of Jesus' death on the cross; and **Easter Monday**, which marks his resurrection. (In Western countries, Easter is typically celebrated on the day before.)

Recipes

Puff-Puff

(Makes 20–30 doughnuts)
1 cup plain flour
Pinch of salt
1 cup water
1/2 cup sugar
2 tsp. yeast
Vegetable oil for frying

Directions:
1. Mix together all of the ingredients except the oil until the dough is smooth.
2. Set the dough aside, in a draft-free place (the inside of an oven that is not turned on works well) until it has risen to about twice its size. This may take about two hours.
3. When the dough has risen, pour 2 inches of oil into a pot and place on low heat.
4. After the oil has heated, carefully drop a small amount of dough into the oil. If the oil is hot enough, the dough ball will rise to the top. When the oil is hot enough, *carefully* drop spoon-sized balls into the oil. Only do a few at a time; if you put too many in the pot the oil will cool off and your puff-puff will be greasy.
5. Fry for a few minutes, then turn them over. Cook until the other side is golden brown. Using a slotted spoon, remove the puff-puff to a paper towel–lined plate. Sprinkle with powdered sugar.

Fried Yam

3 medium yams
Vegetable oil for frying

Directions:
1. Slice the yams into small strips. Try to get them all about the same size. Pour 2 inches of oil into a pot and place on low heat.
2. When the oil is hot (you can test by putting the end of one of the strips in the oil and seeing if it will sizzle), carefully place a few of the strips in the oil, which should completely cover the potatoes.
3. Cook thoroughly, turning as necessary.
4. Using a slotted spoon, remove to a paper towel–lined plate.

Asaro

4 yams
1 small can of tomato paste
1 small can of tomato sauce
1 small onion, chopped
Salt and pepper to taste

Directions:

1. Clean and peel the yams. Cut into 1-inch cubes.
2. Place them in a large pot with water to cover and cook on high.
3. Add the tomato sauce, tomato paste, onions, and salt and pepper. Cook until the yams are soft. This is usually eaten as a side dish.

Obe Ata (Pepper Soup)

16-oz. can of tomato sauce
6-oz. can of tomato paste
1 bell pepper
1 pound of beef cubed or chicken cubed
2 onions, chopped
Salt and Pepper
Palm oil (if available) or vegetable oil
Water

Directions:

1. Place the beef or chicken in a pot with a little water. Add a little salt, and cook until the meat is almost tender.
2. Blend together the tomato sauce and tomato paste, and pour into pot. Add the onions and bell pepper, along with the oil. Cook 20–30 minutes, stirring often.
3. Add salt and pepper to taste.

Dodo

3 ripe plantains
Some vegetable oil

Directions:

1. Put about 1/2 inches of oil into a pan and place on low heat.
2. Slice the plantains so they are about 1/4-inch thick. Try to get them all the same thickness so they will cook at the same rate. Put the plantains into the hot oil and cook until the bottoms are golden brown.
3. Turn and cook until the other side has the same color. Remove to a paper towel–covered plate to drain.

Eat as is, or sprinkle sugar over them.

Glossary

bicameral—a system of government based on two legislative bodies, such as a senate and a house of representatives.

caliphate—a region ruled by a kind of leader called a caliph.

capital resources—goods used to produce other goods.

coalition—a temporary union of distinct bodies working for a single purpose.

coup—a sudden overthrow of a government.

desertification—the process of turning land into a desert, either through land mismanagement or changes in climate.

equatorial—having the characteristics of the area around the equator.

excavated—removed from or dug out of the soil.

genre—a category of art based on form, style, or content.

gross national income (GNI) per capita—the total value of all goods and services produced domestically in a year, supplemented by income received from abroad, divided by midyear population.

infrastructure—the public works (e.g., building, roads, utilities) of an area.

metropolitan—constituting a city and its surrounding area.

mythology—a people's system of beliefs in gods and legendary heroes.

plantain—a starchy fruit, resembling a banana, that is native to the tropics.

savannas—a tropical or subtropical grassland, such as that found in eastern Africa, with scattered trees and plants resistant to drought.

secede—to formally withdraw from an organization or state.

subjugate—to bring a people or nation under control by conquest.

sub-Saharan—existing south of the Sahara Desert in Africa.

subsistence farming—farming that generates only enough produce to support life.

tithe—the payment of a specific fraction (one-tenth) of one's income to someone or to an organization.

tropical—characteristic of a frost-free environment with humidity and high temperatures that provide for year-round plant growth.

vulnerable—exposed or open to attack.

Project and Report Ideas

Reports

Write a brief essay discussing your position on any of the topic sentences below. In your essay, you should briefly introduce the topic, provide evidence that supports your position, and then summarize your thoughts.

- The oil industry has damaged the environment in Nigeria.
- It is important that Nigeria saves the animals in the country that are nearing extinction.
- Nigeria would be an interesting place to visit.
- Racial and ethnic tensions must be eased for Nigeria to reach its potential.

Write a report explaining how the Hausa-Fulani, Igbo, and Yoruba are similar and how they are different.

Investigate what your life would be like as a member of one of Nigeria's ethnic communities. What kind of food would you eat? What types of jobs would you have? Write a one-page report about your discoveries.

Write and give a report on famous Nigerians. Examples include singers Sade and Seal and basketball star Hakeem Olajuwon.

Maps

Draw a map showing Nigerian states and territories. Indicate the climate and geography of the regions.

Select one of the geographical regions of Nigeria and make a map showing the characteristics of the land. If possible, indicate the animals that live in that area.

Project and Report Ideas

Creative Projects

Investigate opportunities to be pen pals (through mail or e-mail) with students your age in Nigeria.

Masks are important in many Nigerian festivals. Make a papier-mâché mask and explain how it would be used in a festival.

Draw the Nigerian flag and underneath the picture, write an explanation of the significance of its colors.

Plan a trip to Nigeria. Get examples of documents you might need (passports, visas, medical certificates, etc.). Prepare your schedule and find or make some images that could be used as postcards.

Experience the Culture

The Internet has Web sites explaining the different types of Nigerian music. Find some audio samples and play them for the class. Explain how Nigerian and other African styles of music have influenced American music.

The yam is an important crop in many parts of Nigeria. There are even festivals to celebrate it. Research what crop is important in region that you live, and in class have a celebration in honor of that crop.

Research the foods that are popular in Nigeria. Check out the recipe section of this book. Select a few and prepare them in class.

Chronology

500 B.C.– **A.D. 200**	Artifacts of the Nok culture are left on the Jos Plateau.
1885	The Oil Rivers Protectorate is established.
1900	The Niger Coast Protectorate joins with the British colony of Lagos and becomes the Protectorate of Southern Nigeria.
1901–1906	The northern half of Nigeria is brought under British control.
1914	The Colony and Protectorate of Nigeria is created.
1951	Britain grants Nigeria self-rule.
1957	Abubakar Tafawa Balewa is appointed prime minister of the new Federation of Nigeria.
1958	The Nigerian armed forces are placed under federal control and the Nigerian navy is established.
1960	In October, Nigeria declares its independence from Britain; Nnamdi Azikiwe becomes governor-general and Balewa retains his position as prime minister.
1963	Nigeria officially becomes a republic; Azikiwe is inaugurated as president.
1966	In a military coup in January, Balewa is assassinated and Azikiwe is removed; another coup later that year places Colonel Yakubu Gowon in power.
1967–70	On July 6, the civil war between the federal government and the Republic of Biafra begins; Biafra surrenders in January 1970.
1971	Nigeria joins Organization of the Petroleum Exporting Countries (OPEC).
1975	Murtala Muhammad replaces Colonel Gowon in bloodless coup.

1976	President Muhammad is assassinated.
1979	The government establishes a new constitution; Alhaji Shehu Shagari becomes the first elected executive president.
1983	Shagari is reelected in September, but the military returns to government through a coup in December.
1991	Abuja officially becomes the new national capital.
1993	Defense Minister Sani Abacha seizes power and institutes a repressive regime.
1998	Abacha dies and is succeeded by Major-General Abdulsalam Abubakar.
1999	Obsanjo is elected president; a new constitution is adopted.
2001	Sharia riots break out over the implementation of Islamic law.
2002	Ethnic fighting takes places in Lagos between Yorubas and Hausas; more than 200 people die in riots in Kaduna over controversy surrounding the Miss World beauty pageant, intended to be held in Abuja.
2003	Nigeria deploys troops to fight in the Liberian Civil War; Obsanjo is reelected president.
2004	The ruling People's Democratic Party sweeps in local elections in March; almost 50 people die in violence at the polls; opponents claim that results were rigged.
2005	Nigeria's president attends the New Partnership for Africa's Development (NEPAD) conference in Egypt.

Further Reading/Internet Resources

Anda, Michael O. *Yoruba.* New York: The Rosen Publishing Group, 1996.

Hamilton, Janice. *Nigeria in Pictures.* Minneapolis, Minn.: Lerner Publishing Group, 2003.

Harmon, Dan E. *Nigeria.* Philadelphia: Chelsea House, 2000.

McIntosh, Gavin. *Hausaland Tales: An Anthology of Folktales from Northern Nigeria.* New Haven, Conn.: Shoe String Press, 2002.

Nnoromele, Salome C., and William Goodwin. *Nigeria.* Farmington Hill, Mich.: Gale Group, 2001.

Ogbaa, Kalu. *Igbo.* New York: The Rosen Publishing Group, 1995.

Travel Information

http://www.lonelyplanet.com/destinations/africa/nigeria
http://www.state.gov/r/pa/ei/bgn/2836.htm
http://www.travel-guide.com/data/nga/nga.asp

History and Geography

http://www.cia.gov/cia/publications/factbook/geos/ni.html
http://www.cyberschoolbus.un.org/infonation/index.asp
http://www.workmall.com/wfb2001/nigeria/nigeria_history_index.html

Economic and Political Information

http://www.usaid.gov/locations/sub-saharan_africa/countries/nigeria
http://www.dfat.gov.au/geo/nigeria

Culture and Festivals

http://www.webinstituteforteachers.org/~esohes/africa/culture.html
http://www.onlinenigeria.com/traditions_Customs.asp

U.S. Embassy, Abuja
7 Mambilla Street
Off Aso Drive, Maitama District
Abuja, Nigeria
(+234) 9-5230916
E-mail: usabuja@state.gov
Web site: http://usembassy.state.gov/nigeria

Embassy of the Federal Republic of Nigeria
3519 International Court, NW
Washington, DC 20008
(202) 986-8400
Fax: (202) 775-1385
Web site: http://www.nigeriaembassyusa.org

Nigeria Tourism Development Corporation
Old Secretariat, Area 1, Garki
P.M.B. 167
Abuja, Nigeria
(+234) 9-2342764
Fax (+234) 9-2342775
Web site: http://www.nigeriatourism.net

Index

Numbers in **bold italic** refer to captions.

Index

Contributors/Picture Credits

Professor Robert I. Rotberg is Director of the Program on Intrastate Conflict and Conflict Resolution at the Kennedy School, Harvard University, and President of the World Peace Foundation. He is the author of a number of books and articles on Africa, including *A Political History of Tropical Africa* and *Ending Autocracy, Enabling Democracy: The Tribulations of Southern Africa*.

Ida Walker has a degree in Museum Studies/Art History from the University of Northern Iowa in Cedar Falls. She did graduate work at Syracuse University. A project manager for a publishing services company and a freelance editor and proofreader, she lives in New York State.